Animal TAILS

Tim Harris

First published in Great Britain in 2019 by Wayland
Copyright © Hodder and Stoughton, 2019

HB ISBN: 978 1 5263 1254 9
PB ISBN: 978 1 5263 1255 6

Printed and bound in Dubai

Editor: Amy Pimperton
Design: Emma DeBanks
Picture research: Rachelle Morris (Nature Picture Library), Diana Morris

Picture credits:
Ardea: Tom & Pat Leeson 37b.
Nature PL: Theo Allofs/Minden 30–31c; Ingo Arndt 38–39c; Eric Baccega 37t; Lucas Bustamente 12r; John Carnemolla 31t; Mark Carwardine 45t; Bernard Castelein 41t; Chris & Monique Fellows 29bl; Wim van den Heever 9; Richard Herrmann/Minden 28–29c; Daniel Heuclin 12cb; J-L Klein & M-L Hubert 32; M & C Denis-Huot 34; Jabruson 11tr; Donald M Jones 14–15c; Sebastian Kennerknecht 33c; Michael D Kern 22–23c, 45b, 46tr; Heiko Kiera 23t; Pascal Kobeh 26bl; Tim Laman 18–19c; Chien Lee 16–17c; Remi Masson 21bl; Bence Máté 8; Alexander Mustard 26-27c; Cheryl-Samantha Owen 35b; Pete Oxford/Minden 27tl; David Pattyn front cover bl, 19tl; Tony Phelps 24; Mark Raycroft/Minden: 36; Andy Rouse 4–5c; Philip A Savoie 15b; Kim Taylor 2,17b; Richard du Toit 44–45c; Theo Webb 19cr; Winfried Wisniewski/Minden 35t.
Shutterstock: Ali Ayoob Photography 5c; bartuchna@yahoo.pl 16b; John Bell front cover tr; Jan Bures front cover br; Captivelight 3, 11b; Vinod V Chandran 7tr; Cathy Withers-Clarke 39b; Iain Clyne 33b; Danita Delmont 4t; Iian Ejzkowicz 43bl; NickEvansKZN 27br; EvgenySHCH 6r; Mirko Graul 15t; Frode Jacobsen 14br; JPL Designs 11tl; Holger Kirk 25c; Mees Kuiper 38bc; Andrew Linscott 39t; Edmund Lowe Photography 42b; Thomas Marent 10r; Mark Medcalf 6bc; megablaster 29tr; David Montreuil 19b; Neofelizz 42–43c; Nico99 43cr; Erwin Niemand 33t; Jay Ondriecka 21tr; Alta Oosthuizen 20c; Andrew Parkinson 40; Ben Queenborough 46bl; Damian Ryszawy 44b; SergeUWPhoto 13t; Simon Shim 25t; shymar27 23b; Stavrida 41c; 2630ben 46br; Tsekhmister front cover tl, back cover bl; Colin Robert Varndell 7br; YK 41b; Milan Zygmunt 6–7c,13b.

Wayland, an imprint of
Hachette Children's Group
Part of Hodder and Stoughton
Carmelite House
50 Victoria Embankment
London EC4Y 0DZ

An Hachette UK Company

www.hachette.co.uk
www.hachettechildrens.co.uk

MIX
Paper from
responsible sources
FSC® C104740
FSC
www.fsc.org

Contents

A world of tails

The variety of tails in the animal kingdom is staggering. Some monkeys have very long tails, squirrels and foxes have bushy ones and peacocks have enormous and incredibly colourful tails.

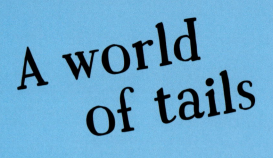
Zebra swallowtail

What is a tail? ➤

A tail sticks out from the end of a body. Most are bendy and many taper to a point. It is usually vertebrate animals that have tails, but a few invertebrates, such as scorpions and butterflies, have them, too.

A peacock's huge tail is an impressive sight!

Mojave rattlesnake

Useful tails ↑

Why do so many animals have a tail? Are they just for decoration or are there other reasons? Tails are important for animals in many different ways, such as helping them balance in trees, showing off to mates, defending themselves against predators (like the rattlesnake above) or guiding their young. You'll be amazed at just how useful a tail can be!

Tails for balance

Squirrels eat seeds, nuts, berries and tender green shoots. To reach these foods they have to climb high into the tree canopy and walk along narrow twigs and branches. Their long, bushy tails help them to balance. If a squirrel starts to tip to one side, it moves its tail the other way to balance the force of gravity that is pulling it down towards the ground.

Parachute ➡

As a squirrel leaps from tree to tree the wide, fluffy tail creates drag – a bit like a parachute – slowing the animal down for landing.

Red squirrel

A red squirrel's tail is almost as long as its head and body.

Indian giant squirrels grow to 1 metre long, with more than half of that length being tail!

Indian giant squirrel

← The high life

A long tail also helps other tree-living animals, such as red pandas, to keep their balance. Red pandas live in forests in the Himalayas where they eat mainly bamboo, as well as berries, flowers and even small birds. They would have a pretty tough life if they kept falling out of trees!

Red panda

Wood mouse

A wood mouse has a long, thin tail. Its sense of balance is so good that it can run quickly along thin branches without falling off.

Balancing at speed

A double-crested basilisk lizard can do something completely awesome. To escape a predator, it can run on water! This lizard, sometimes called a 'Jesus Christ lizard', paddles its hind legs furiously and holds its tail above the water. This helps to stop the lizard from falling in!

A double-crested basilisk lizard (or Jesus Christ lizard) can run more than 10 metres over water.

⬅ Fast food

Some animals have a tail that helps them change direction at high speed. A cheetah needs to sprint to catch speedy prey, such as antelopes. An antelope will zig-zag when it is trying to escape and the cheetah follows its every twist and turn. As it turns to the left, the cheetah switches its tail to the right to keep its balance; as it turns to the right, the tail is flicked to the left.

Springbok and cheetah

Cheetahs are the fastest land animals, able to reach 120 kph, but only for short distances. Without a tail, they would fall over when changing direction at speed.

Prehensile tails

A spider monkey is a primate with very long arms and legs and a very special tail. Its flexible tip is covered with ridges of skin and can grasp hold of branches, almost like an extra hand. A tail that grabs like this is called prehensile. Not all primates have prehensile tails.

Speedy swinging ➡

Spider monkeys use their long tail to balance when walking along a branch. But it is most useful for leaving their hands free to grasp food that is hard to reach or when they are racing at speed through the highest branches of trees.

A black-faced spider monkey uses its tail as it feeds high in the canopy.

Mastering the art of hanging by the tail is an important skill for juvenile (young) black howler monkeys. (Only the males have black fur; females and juveniles have pale fur.)

Black howler monkey (juvenile)

Tree pangolin

In the forests of West Africa, scaly tree pangolins climb trees in search of insect food. These animals use their tail to grab hold of branches as they move.

Harvest mouse

← Climbing high

A tiny harvest mouse uses its prehensile tail to help it clamber up twigs and among the stalks of tall grasses. Unlike the rest of the animal, the tip of the tail is not furry, which helps with better grip.

Tails for gripping

All snakes have a tail, but it's hard to know where it starts because the whole animal is long and thin. Some tree-living snakes have a prehensile tail (see pages 10–11), allowing them to hang from branches as they slither around in search of prey. Emerald tree boas are expert at hanging on by their tail when searching for a tasty morsel to eat.

The tree-dwelling monkey-tailed skink has a prehensile tail that makes up more than half the animal's length.

Monkey-tailed skink

← Hold tight

Seahorses also have tails that grip. These little creatures are fish, not swimming horses! Seahorses are not strong swimmers and can easily be swept away by ocean currents. To remain in the same place, they use their long tail to grip hold of underwater plants or coral.

Denise's pygmy seahorse

Lifeline →

When it lunges for insect prey, a chameleon's feet sometimes let go of the branch it was standing on. Only its prehensile tail, wrapped around the branch, keeps it from falling to the ground.

Panther chameleon

A juvenile emerald tree boa is orange, not green. It will turn green when it becomes an adult.

Tails for flight

A pilot controls a rudder to steer a plane through the air and birds do something similar. They twist or spread the tail feathers to change direction.

Pirate birds →

Frigatebirds are 'pirates' of the ocean, snatching fish from the water and chasing other seabirds to force them to cough up their last meal – then swallowing it themselves! They need to change direction super-fast and that's why their tail is so important. A frigatebird is constantly moving the muscles in its deeply forked tail to help the twisting, turning pursuit of its unlucky victim.

Frigatebirds change the position of their long, narrow wings as well as their tail to change direction in flight.

Frigatebird (with closed tail)

➤ In pursuit

Swallows are another bird with a deeply forked tail. It helps them twist and turn quicky as they pursue flying insect prey.

Barn swallow

Red kite

Red kites are birds of prey that often soar in the air as they scan the ground below for food. They twist their tail feathers to help turn to the left or right when they are flying.

Tails for gliding

Flying fish are incredible speedsters, capable of travelling through the air at more than 70 kph. Before they launch themselves from the water – usually to escape predatory fish – they vibrate their tail from side to side more than 50 times a second to gain speed. Then they shoot out of the water and glide with their fins stuck out like the wings of a plane.

Flying fish can travel through the air for up to 350 metres. Just before they touch down again they start to flick their tail rapidly once more.

A flying fish keeps its tail still while it is gliding. It only starts to vibrate it again just before it touches down in the water.

Flying fish

Expert gliders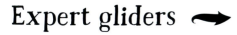

Flying squirrels are amazing forest creatures. They are capable of gliding 90 metres from one tree to another because they have webs of skin, called patagia, between their front and back legs, and a long bushy tail.

When stretched, the patagia turn the animal into a glider and the tail acts as a rudder and air brake. By changing the position of its tail, the squirrel can veer right or left in flight. Before coming in to land on a tree trunk, it raises the tail to act as an air brake.

Flying squirrel

Since they can glide from tree to tree, flying squirrels can get around more quickly than many other forest mammals.

Tails for showing off

Lots of birds have tails to impress potential partners. The male Wilson's bird of paradise performs a dance on the forest floor to impress the female. As he dances, he displays his extraordinary tail, which curls into two violet spirals.

The female watches the dance from above to see the male's impressive colours from the best angle. As he dances, the iridescent tail feathers shimmer and appear to change colour as they catch the light.

A male Wilson's bird of paradise has vivid plumage to attract females.

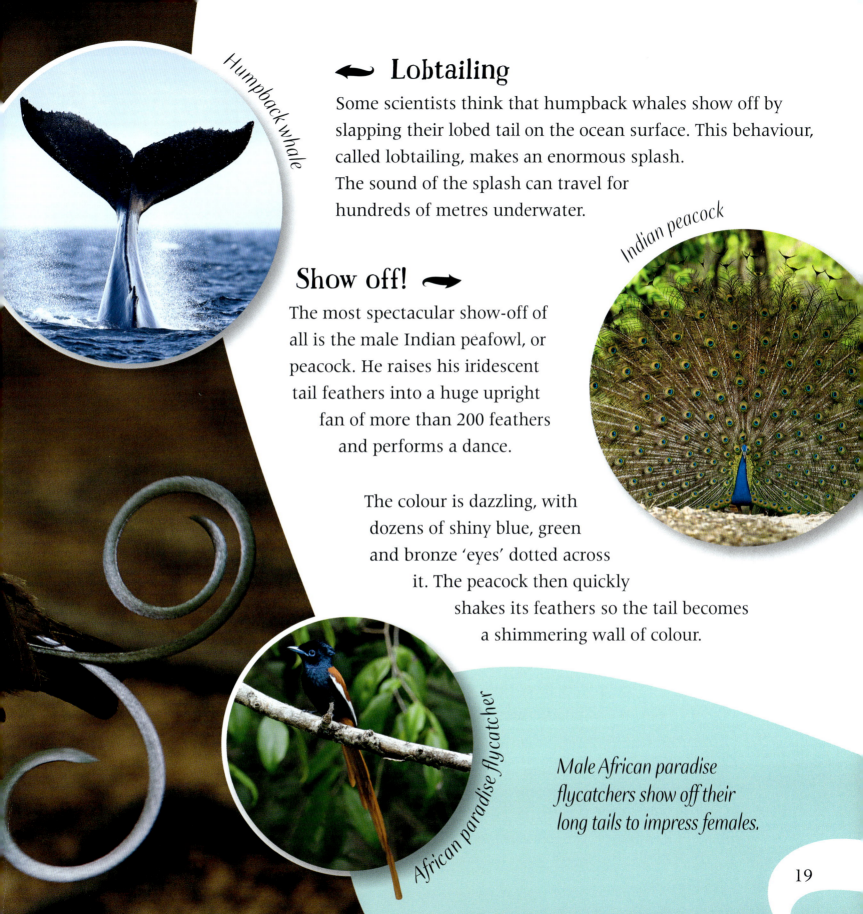

← Lobtailing

Some scientists think that humpback whales show off by slapping their lobed tail on the ocean surface. This behaviour, called lobtailing, makes an enormous splash. The sound of the splash can travel for hundreds of metres underwater.

Humpback whale

Show off! →

The most spectacular show-off of all is the male Indian peafowl, or peacock. He raises his iridescent tail feathers into a huge upright fan of more than 200 feathers and performs a dance.

Indian peacock

The colour is dazzling, with dozens of shiny blue, green and bronze 'eyes' dotted across it. The peacock then quickly shakes its feathers so the tail becomes a shimmering wall of colour.

African paradise flycatcher

Male African paradise flycatchers show off their long tails to impress females.

19

Tails for keeping cool

Fur and feathers insulate mammals and birds to keep them warm in freezing winter weather. That may be a problem in summer though, when very hot weather means the animals may overheat. It may seem strange that some animals can use their tails to keep cool, but that is exactly what some do.

Parasol ➡

Tails can be used in a variety of ways to overcome this problem. Cape ground squirrels live out in the open in parts of southern Africa. On hot, sunny days they use their tail as a parasol to shade their head and body from the full glare of the sun.

A Cape ground squirrel turns its back to the sun and flicks its tail over its head – instant parasol!

Cold blood ➡

An animal's blood moves heat from one part of its body to another. Snakes are called 'cold-blooded' animals. They don't create their own heat, but depend on the warmth of their surroundings. On very hot days, garter snakes have a clever way of cooling off: they pump more blood into their tail, allowing more heat to leave the snake's body through its skin.

Common garter snake

⬅ Furless tails

Beavers have a cool way of dealing with the heat, other than spending time in freshwater pools. Their broad, flat, paddle-shaped tail doesn't have any fur, so it loses heat more quickly than the animal's furry body.

European beaver

Warning tails

Many animals use their tail as a warning. Squirrels will flick theirs to alert other squirrels if they spot a predator. Cats will swish their tails to let you know that they want you to back off.

Although rattlesnakes are armed with fangs and deadly venom, they also have an awesome tail defence. The snake has four or five 'buttons' at the tip of its tail. When these are shaken they make a rattling warning sound. When a coyote or person comes too close, the snake lifts the tip of its tail, shakes its rattle and – alarmed – the intruder retreats.

This red diamondback rattlesnake is coiled up in a defensive posture as it rattles its tail.

Timber rattlesnake rattle

← How old?

Rattles grow as the snake gets older. A new rattle segment is added each time the snake sheds its skin. However, you can't tell how old a snake is from the number of segments, as they are very delicate and often break off.

↓ Fluff it out

Have you ever noticed what a cat does if it feels threatened, perhaps by a dog? It raises its tail and fluffs the hairs out to make itself look bigger.

Domestic cat

When a cat is scared, muscles at the base of each hair follicle contract, pulling the hair upright – a bit like when humans get goosebumps and the hairs on their skin stand on end.

Tails for attack

Some insects and other invertebrates have stingers at the end of their tail, through which they deliver venom to paralyse their prey. Scorpions have two grasping pincers, eight legs and a long, segmented tail, which is usually curved over their back.

Toxic tip ➤

At the tip of the tail is a sharp stinger, called a telson. When a scorpion finds prey, such as a worm, centipede or small mouse, it stabs the telson into its victim and quickly pumps a toxic mix of chemicals into its prey, so it can't move.

The granulated thick-tailed scorpion is one of the most venomous species in southern Africa.

A scorpion's telson contains two glands in which venom is stored, and two tiny tubes, through which the venom is pumped when the scorpion attacks.

Telson

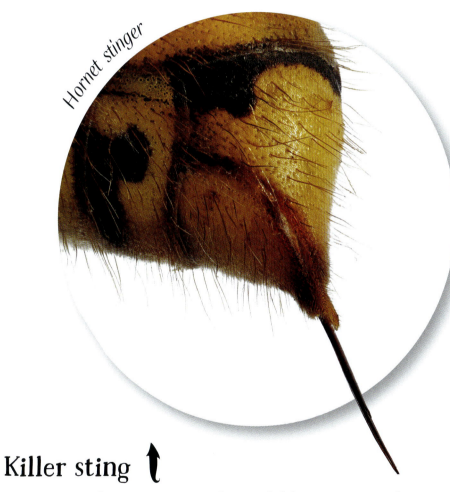

Hornet stinger

Killer sting ↑

Hornets are large wasps with a tail-like stinger at the tip of their abdomen (the rearmost section of an insect's body). They stab their stinger into insects as large as honeybees, paralysing them before eating them.

25

Tails for defence

Tails can be useful in a number of ways to protect an animal. Stingrays are not generally aggressive fish, but do use venom to defend themselves. If a stingray is threatened it will flip its long tail up and over its body to strike whatever is in front of it. The sharp dermal ray (stinger) enters the attacker's flesh and venom is squirted into it.

A stringray's dermal ray is up to 20 cm long and has jagged edges, so when it is pulled out, it tears the flesh of its attacker.

Black-spotted stingray (dermal ray)

Brazilian three-banded armadillo

← Roll up

Armadillos are mammals that live in North and South America. Most of their body is covered with protective scales, which are a good defence against predators. However, the armadillo's face is not scaly, so is vulnerable to attack. When threatened, an armadillo will roll up into a ball with its scaly tail covering its face.

These lizards get their name from their habit of clasping their tail in their mouth and rolling into a ball, a little like an armadillo. They do this when they are startled.

Armadillo girdled lizard

Tails for swimming

Most fish move through water by swishing their tails from side to side. Some can swim very fast. The yellowfin tuna is a large fish, growing more than 2 metres long. It is one of the fastest fish and can reach an awesome 75 kph.

A yellowfin's strong muscles power its large, crescent-shaped tail, flicking it from side to side to push it forwards. Speed is important for tuna because they need to cover vast distances: they migrate hundreds of kilometres between rich feeding areas and the places where they breed.

The yellowfin tuna's crescent-shaped tail propels it rapidly through water.

28

American crocodile

Stealth swimmers ⬆

It is not just fish that use their tails to swim. Crocodiles move their powerful tails in a wave-like motion from side-to-side. This helps them to glide stealthily through the water as they patiently hunt for prey.

Shortfin mako shark

The predatory shortfin mako shark is another very fast fish, capable of swimming at 74 kph in short bursts.

Tails for walking

When kangaroos bound across the Australian Outback on their hind legs, their short front legs don't touch the ground, and their tail is held out behind them for balance. Kangaroos don't race around most of the time, though. They spend much of their time walking slowly as they graze.

Pentapedal

Kangaroos walk on all four legs and they also use their tail as a fifth 'leg' to push themselves forwards. This kind of movement is called pentapedal ('penta' means five).

The extra support of a tail comes in handy for a female red kangaroo carrying her joey (baby).

Red kangaroo

Kangaroos can hop at 70 kph. Their tail trailing behind them helps them stay balanced at speed.

31

Tails as props

Some animals use their tail as an additional means of support when they stand tall on their back legs. This is called the tripod stance, and it means the animal is less likely to topple over. Meerkats, kangaroos and some birds are among the animals that adopt this position.

Stretching tall to get a better view of what's going on in the world, this meerkat is using its tail as a third 'leg'.

Standing sentry ➡

Meerkats live in large groups, but are at risk of attack by predators, such as eagles and jackals. Several meerkats stand sentry to watch over the group and they use the tripod stance to see as far and high as possible.

Meerkats

⬇ Fighting stance

When kangaroos are 'boxing' to establish dominance, their tails help them keep their balance. In a similar way, Komodo dragons also use their tails to help them fight rivals for food and mates.

The stiff feathers of a treecreeper's tail keep it from falling backwards as it climbs a tree trunk.

Red kangaroos (boxing)

Treecreeper

33

Tails as guides

A leopard is a big cat with a long tail. Its sand-coloured fur is covered with black markings, called rosettes, making the animal hard to spot in tall grass or shaded forest. Most of the time, it suits a leopard not to be noticed – after all, it doesn't want to be seen by its prey.

However, when a female leopard has cubs there's a danger they might lose sight of her and get lost. But the tip of her tail has a splash of bright white fur on the underside. When she raises the tail and curls the tip over, the white acts like a sign for the cubs to follow.

An African leopard cub follows its mother's tail.

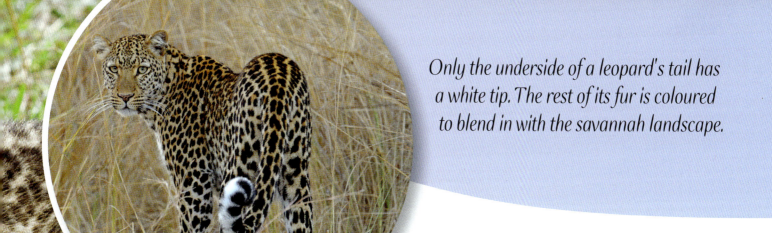

Only the underside of a leopard's tail has a white tip. The rest of its fur is coloured to blend in with the savannah landscape.

African leopard

Hold on ➥

Elephants are very social animals and form strong bonds with their herd. An elephant calf will often hold the tail of its mother or another older elephant, in order to keep up with the herd as it moves between feeding grounds.

African elephant calf

Tails for communicating

Many mammals have their own 'tail language'. The position and movement of their tail sends messages to others of their kind: telling of danger, warning to stay away or signalling attraction.

When a white-tailed deer spies a wolf prowling nearby in the forest, its tail adopts the 'flag' position. It is raised upright to show the white fur beneath. This is a sign to other deer in the herd to run away.

This white-tailed deer is holding its tail in the 'flag' position.

Social signals ➜

Canines, such as domestic dogs and wolves, have many ways of expressing their moods – whether they are happy, miserable, angry or afraid. A happy canine is likely to hold its tail at medium height and wag it from side to side, but an angry canine holds its tail high, stiff and erect. A tail tucked between the legs is a signal that the animal is worried about something.

European grey wolf

North American beaver

When a beaver is alarmed it slaps its tail hard on the water, making a loud splash, to warn other beavers of danger.

Fly-swatting tails

Have you ever noticed a group of horses or cattle swishing their tails in unison? The chances are that they are doing this to keep pesky flies away. In many parts of the world, flies aren't just annoying – they also carry diseases, so it is important for animals, such as giraffes, elephants, horses, zebras and even leopards to swat the flies before they bite.

When a giraffe swings its tail, the tuft of black hairs at the end sweeps insects off its rump. Adult giraffes have the longest tail of any land mammal; it may grow to 2.4 metres.

Masai giraffe

There are two parts to a zebra's tail: the dock and the skirt. The dock is the skin and muscles covering the tail vertebrae (bones), and the skirt is made up of the long hairs that hang below the dock.

Zebra

← Swish and flick

The tails of these animals have two pivots, or turning points – one where the tail joins the animal's rump, and one where the bony part of the tail ends. When the animal swishes its tail, the long hairs at the end flick faster than the bony section and can even swish in a slightly different direction – making it a more effective weapon against unwelcome flies.

African elephant

The thickest hairs on an elephant grow from the end of its tail. They are perfect for sweeping away mosquitoes and other flying insects.

Tails for marking territory

Especially during the breeding season, many mammals spray urine or poo around their territory to warn other animals to keep away. This is called scent marking. So that their scent covers as wide an area as possible, hippos spin their tails around like a ship's propeller when they are defecating (doing a poo). The spinning tail scatters strong-smelling poo over a wide area, saving the animal from doing so much walking!

A hippo's tail is not long, but it is good for spreading poo.

⬅ Scent marking

On the African island of Madagascar, ring-tailed lemurs hold their boldly striped tails out straight when they are scent marking their territory with urine.

Ring-tailed lemur

Ring-tailed lemur (rubbing its arms on its tail)

Pygmy hippo

Ring-tailed lemurs engage in 'stink fights' with rival lemurs. Each lemur rubs scent from its arms on to its tail and waves the tail in the face of its opponent!

Hippos' smaller cousins, pygmy hippos, also perform the tail-spinning trick.

Tails that drop off

Tails are useful, but they can also cause problems. For one thing, they are easy for predators to grasp hold of. Some animals get around this problem in an extraordinary way. Lizards, such as skinks, geckos and salamanders, can shed their tail if it is grabbed by a predator.

Two of the tail bones become 'unhitched' and the tail drops off! Sometimes it still wiggles on the ground for a few seconds after it has come away. Incredibly, a new tail can grow back again, although this may take several weeks.

This common sun skink has lost its tail, but the animal will be able to lead a near-normal life until it grows back.

Common sun skink

A colourful day gecko climbs a wall.

This gecko once lost its tail. The muscles, blood vessels and skin regrew, but the tiny tail bones have been replaced by elastic tissue called cartilage.

Mediterranean house gecko

← Escape!

When a fox, snake or owl grabs the tail of a spiny mouse, the skin comes away in the predator's mouth, allowing the mouse to escape. The mouse doesn't lose the whole of its tail and it later eats the muscle and bone that is left, leaving it with a short tail – or no tail at all.

Spiny mouse

Big, long and unusual tails

There are some big, long and unusual tails in the animal kingdom. Male long-tailed widow birds (right), which live in African grasslands, have a tail that is four times longer than their body!

Camouflage →

Leaf-tailed geckos are nocturnal hunters. By day, they hide in bushes and trees. They mimic (copy) leaves with their unusual leaf-shaped and patterned bodies and tails to avoid detection from predators.

Satanic leaf-tailed gecko

Blue whales are the largest animals on Earth; their tail flukes measure up to 8 metres across.

Asian grass lizards have a tail three times their body length.

Blue whale

Asian grass lizard

45

Activities to try

Make a rattlesnake's tail ➡

Thread 10 or 12 buttons on to string or strong thread. Tie them together, but don't tie them too tight. Give them a gentle shake. This is how the rattle at the end of a rattlesnake's tail works.

⬇ Balancing act

Try walking along a low balance beam without any help.* Do it again holding a very long wooden ruler. There should be an equal amount of ruler to your left and to your right. Which is easier? This is the same principle used by animals when they are balancing.

*Ask an adult to supervise you.

Make up your own tail language

Imagine you and your friends each have a tail – and that you are going to communicate with each other using the position of your tail and its movement. You can lower it to the ground, raise it high, wag it from side to side, or up and down. Make up a tail language to describe your moods. ➡

Glossary

air brake a moveable flap on an aircraft used to reduce speed

canopy the layer of branches and leaves of trees in a forest

contract when a muscle becomes shorter and tighter in order to move another part of the body

coral a hard material made from the skeletons of some marine invertebrates

crest skin or feathers that stick up from the head or back of an animal

dermal from the layer below the outer skin of an animal

fluke the broad, flat parts of a whale's tail

follicle the cells and tissue around the root of a hair

Himalayas a huge mountain range in Asia

insulate to protect something from heat or cold

invertebrate animal without a backbone; snails, spiders, and insects are all invertebrates

iridescent bright colours that seem to change colour when seen from different angles

mammals warm-blooded animal with hair or fur that drinks its mother's milk when young

morsel a small piece of food

nocturnal active at night

paralyse to cause the whole body (or part of a body) to become unable to move

pirate a person who attacks and robs ships at sea

plumage a bird's feathers

predator animal that hunts and eats other animals

prehensile tail or tongue that is flexible and able to hold objects, such as a branch

prey animal that is eaten by other animals

primate a mammal, such as humans, monkeys, lemurs, apes and lorises

reptile cold-blooded animal with dry scaly skin

rudder a flat, hinged flap on a plane or boat that helps with steering

rump the back end of an animal

savannah grassy plains in tropical and sub-tropical parts of the world

segmented divided into parts

stealthily moving quietly so as not to be seen or heard

territory an area defended by an animal

toxic poisonous

tripod three-legged

unison performing an action at the same time

veer to change direction suddenly

venom poisonous liquid made by animals, such as spiders

vertebrate animal with a backbone; mammals, birds, fish, amphibians and reptiles are vertebrates

vivid very bright or deep colours

Further information

Books

Animal Superheroes by Raphaël Martin (Wayland, 2016)

Animal Tongues by Tim Harris (Wayland, 2019)

The Poo That Animals Do by Paul Mason and illustrated by Tony De Saulles (Wayland, 2018)

The Wee That Animals Pee by Paul Mason and illustrated by Tony De Saulles (Wayland, 2019)

Wildlife Worlds (series) by Tim Harris (Franklin Watts, 2019)

Index